Woman Tips for the First-Time Groom

Written by a Woman. For Men. About Women. You've Been Warned.

Printed in the United States of America
First Edition: 2025
ISBN: 9798284323830

Table of Contents

Introduction

Welcome to the Emotional Jungle Gym (And Congrats, You Married a Woman)

So... you did it.

You stood in front of your friends, your family, a vaguely sweaty officiant, and the most beautiful woman you've ever seen in your life—and you said those two magical words: "I do."

Now what?

Now you wake up next to a person who cries during pet food commercials, owns 17 types of lotion, and somehow expects you to "just know" what she means when she says, "It's not about the dishes."

You've entered a new world, friend. And spoiler: you are **not** in charge here.

Now don't panic. You're not doomed. You're just... wildly underprepared.

The good news is, you're not alone. Every newly married man walks into this thing armed with confidence, testosterone, and exactly zero practical tools for understanding women. You probably thought being a husband meant taking out the trash, remembering your anniversary, and occasionally agreeing that yes, those pants *do* make her butt look amazing.

Turns out, that's about 4% of the job.

The rest? It's a nonstop, ever-shifting, emotionally nuanced rollercoaster that you were not trained for. You're now the co-owner of a life with someone who experiences time, memory, and tone of voice completely differently than you. You married a creature who doesn't *just* want you to listen—she wants you to absorb, interpret, and emotionally validate while also unloading the dishwasher *the right way*, without being asked.

You thought you were signing up for love and companionship. And you were. But also: feelings. Layers. Subtext. Throw pillows. A complex, beautiful, maddening woman who can both adore you and rage-clean a bathroom because you used her bath towel to wipe up dog pee.

This book is not a list of things to do. She can make that for you herself (and trust me, she will). This is a translation guide. A flashlight. A slightly sarcastic, very honest cheat sheet from a woman who's been where your wife is, thought what she's thinking, and muttered

"Seriously?" under her breath more times than you want to know.

I'm not here to shame you. I'm here to save you—from the confusion, the missteps, the slow emotional erosion that happens when a man loves a woman but has no idea how to actually *live* with her.

We're going to talk about moods. Memory. Mystery towels. Why she cries when she's mad and laughs when she's tired. Why "Just tell me what you want" never works. Why helping is not the same as partnering. And why, despite all her quirks, contradictions, and expectations... she still chose *you*.

If you're still reading, congratulations. You're one of the good ones. Or at least one of the ones who *wants* to be good. That's enough to get started.

Now grab a drink. Sit down. And maybe—just this once—actually listen.

Because I'm about to tell you the stuff she *wishes* she could, but doesn't know how to say without sounding mean.

Let's begin.
(And yes, this time, it's really about the dishes.)

1: She's Not Like You

(Stop Trying to Understand Her Like She Is)

Let's get this out of the way, early and unvarnished: the woman you married does not think like you, act like you, process like you, or recover from conflict like you. She's not emotionally misconfigured, she's not being dramatic, and she doesn't need to "calm down" — and the sooner you stop treating her like a slightly more complicated version of yourself, the fewer times you'll find yourself wondering why she's giving you the silent treatment while slamming drawers hard enough to register on a seismograph.

She's not like you. That's not a complaint. That's not an insult. That's the whole point. But if you keep approaching her through the lens of male logic and masculine emotional strategy, you're going to crash into her reality like a truck full of dirty laundry you forgot was supposed to be folded yesterday.

If this sounds dramatic, buckle up. It gets more confusing from here.

What You Think Is Simple, Isn't

When your wife says, "I feel like I'm doing everything," what you might hear is a slight exaggeration. You start doing a mental checklist — *I vacuumed. I took the dog out. I cooked Tuesday. We both work. What is she talking about?*

And while you're thinking through all of that, she's standing there wondering why you need to itemize anything instead of just saying, "You're right. That sounds exhausting. What do you need from me right now?"

Because she didn't bring it up for a scorecard. She brought it up because she's feeling depleted. She wants partnership, not a printout. And when you jump into justifying your actions, you're sending her a message — whether you mean to or not — that her exhaustion is up for debate. That she needs to "prove" she's allowed to be frustrated.

You think you're explaining. She hears invalidating.

See the gap?

You've Been Trained Differently

Most men weren't raised to examine emotions. You were raised to recognize danger, solve problems, win games, and get stuff done. No one pulled you aside to say, "Hey, when your wife is overwhelmed, sit down and let her vent without defending yourself." That wasn't in gym class. It sure wasn't in college.

So now, you're facing a woman who doesn't always say exactly what she means, because what she means is often layered in tone, timing, mood, hormones, and the context of three previous conversations that you forgot but she's still processing.

And it's maddening. It really is. Especially when you're trying. You're showing up. You're listening (or at least, you're nodding while wondering if this might lead to sex later). But somehow, your good intentions keep hitting a wall.

It's not because she's impossible. It's because she's operating on a different frequency. And if you want to stay married, you're going to have to learn how to hear it — not just tolerate it, but actually *understand* what it means.

No, You're Not Being "Controlled"

Let's talk about this common male fear, just to get it out in the open.

At some point in your first year of marriage, you're going to feel like you're being trained. She'll start asking you to do things a certain way — load the dishwasher differently, fold the towels with the edge in, use the cutting board instead of slicing cheese directly on the counter like a psychopath. And you're going to feel this little flare of rebellion bubble up inside you.

"Am I allowed to do anything my way?"
"Is this what marriage is — getting corrected for breathing wrong?"

No. This is what marriage is: coexisting with someone who has standards, habits, and emotional expectations that *aren't yours.* That's not control. That's partnership. And if you're equating every request or correction with some kind of power grab, that's your ego talking — not her tone of voice.

She's not trying to run your life. She's trying to build a life with you that doesn't feel like she's the only adult in the room. If she wanted a roommate who did everything half-assed and shrugged a lot, she could've stayed single and adopted a golden retriever.

She Wants to Be Understood, Not Managed

This is a subtle shift, but it matters. She doesn't need you to manage her moods like they're maintenance issues. She doesn't need you to smooth things over, redirect, or use logic to get her to "see it your way." That's what you do when your friend won't split the check evenly. It's not how you love a woman.

She needs you to pay attention.

Not all the time. Not perfectly. But enough to notice when she says, "I'm just tired," and what she really means is, "I'm stretched too thin and I feel alone in this." Enough to catch the change in her voice when she says she's "fine," and realize you're being invited — awkwardly, maybe — to ask a follow-up question instead of accepting the out and going back to your phone.

This is not about walking on eggshells. It's about knowing that when you live with someone who feels deeply and often communicates indirectly, your job is to stay attuned — not to anticipate her every whim, but to stop acting surprised that she has them in the first place.

She Will Remember What You Forgot

Here's something you probably didn't think about before getting married: your wife keeps an invisible ledger. Not just of offenses, but of emotions. Of conversations. Of promises. Of tone. Of things you said quickly but she sat with for three days wondering if you meant more by it.

You're going to forget stuff. Appointments. Birthdays. That thing she told you while you were half-asleep. She'll remember it all. And not because she's keeping score, but because she's biologically wired to track the emotional landscape in a way you are not. She's paying attention to your patterns. Not because she wants to trap you — but because she's building context. She's asking herself: *Is he safe? Is he reliable? Is he going to grow with me, or against me?*

You're not under surveillance. You're being felt. Which is worse, in some ways, because you can't lie your way through it. She knows when your heart's not in it. She knows when you're giving the minimum. She knows when you're hiding behind "I'm just tired" because you don't want to talk.

And yeah, it's a lot. But if you stop seeing it as pressure, and start seeing it as a call to show up — not as a perfect husband, but as a present one — then you're on the right track.

Not Better or Worse — Just Different

Somewhere along the way, you're going to be tempted to think she's making things harder than they need to be. That she's overreacting. That she's taking things too personally. That if she would just calm down, everything would be fine.

Maybe. Or maybe what she's doing is *reacting appropriately* to things you've been trained to ignore. Maybe her sensitivity isn't the problem — maybe it's her radar, and you're just now realizing you've been flying blind for most of your life.

You don't have to agree with every feeling she has. You don't have to memorize every emotional cue. But you do need to *respect* the fact that she's wired differently than you — and that it's not your job to teach her how to react more like you.

She doesn't need to be "more chill." You need to be more aware.

This adjustment — learning how she operates, and adjusting to it without losing yourself or becoming resentful — is the first and hardest part of being married to a woman. Not just any woman — *your* woman. With her exact history, her wiring, her wounds, her expectations.

She's not going to change into a simpler version of herself just because you're overwhelmed. And she shouldn't have to.

That's not the deal you signed up for.

And this chapter isn't your solution — it's your warning shot.

What you do next, what you pay attention to, and how you respond when it feels like she's speaking an entirely different language — that's the beginning of your real education.

And there's a lot more coming.

2: The Emotional Weather Report

(How to Read Her Emotional Forecast Before You Step in It)

If you've ever asked your wife, "Are you okay?" and she responded with a clipped "I'm fine" while clearly looking like she wanted to throw a coffee mug through a wall, welcome. You've just stepped into the swirling weather system that is the female emotional forecast. And if you walked away thinking, *well, she said she's fine*, then you also walked away from your chance to handle it with any grace whatsoever.

Marriage comes with many skills no one teaches you. Reading the emotional weather is one of them. It doesn't come naturally to most men. That's not an insult — it's training. Or rather, the lack of it. Boys aren't raised to monitor emotions in real time. You were probably encouraged to manage frustration by pushing it down, ignore tears unless you were bleeding, and treat anger like a gasoline can — dangerous, explosive, and best kept sealed.

She had a different upbringing. Whether her household was calm or chaotic, she was almost certainly taught to monitor the room, pick up on cues, and keep emotional peace. She learned to sense mood shifts before anyone said a word. She learned that sometimes you don't say what you're feeling — you signal. And maybe you wait. Maybe you suppress. Or maybe you find subtle ways to get your needs met without saying the full thing out loud.

Now the two of you live together. And she brings all that internal barometric pressure into your shared space, while you're still standing there wondering why she suddenly got quiet halfway through dinner.

The worst part is, she probably didn't plan on testing you. This isn't some manipulative game she's playing. It's just how she's been conditioned to operate in relationships — especially ones where she's unsure how safe she is to speak plainly. That's where you come in. Not as her decoder or therapist, but as someone who's supposed to care enough to notice.

Let's be fair. Some days, "I'm fine" really means "I'm fine." But most days, especially if she delivers it with that signature tight smile, narrowed eyes, or clipped tone, it's not confirmation — it's a placeholder. It's a signal that something's off and she doesn't want to explain it to someone who's already half-checked out. And yes, she noticed the way you asked. She caught the flicker of impatience in your voice. She heard your footstep as you turned to leave the room before the words were even fully out of her mouth.

Most men back off at this point. You figure: *if she doesn't want to talk, I'm not going to force it.* And that seems reasonable — you were taught to respect boundaries. But she doesn't interpret your exit as respect. She interprets it as abandonment. As confirmation that when she isn't cheerful, agreeable, or "easy," you'd rather disengage.

Now you're both frustrated. You think you gave her space. She thinks you left her in the middle of an emotional house fire with no hose. And the kicker is, neither of you is technically wrong. You're just using different definitions of what "showing up" means.

This is the kind of thing that seems small but snowballs. You're going to have a hundred moments like this in your first year of marriage — and many more after that. The tiny disconnects where one of you thinks, *I handled that well,* and the other thinks, *He didn't even try.* If you're not paying attention, they'll start to define the relationship. Not all at once. Just gradually, like emotional sediment that settles into the foundation and hardens into resentment.

There's a better way to handle it. It starts with learning how to stay in the room.

You don't need to pry. You don't need to ask the same question three times in a row. But if she says "I'm fine" in that voice — and you'll learn it; every woman's is different — you don't walk away. You stay. You sit down. You ask again later. Or you just say, "Okay, but if you want to talk about it later, I'm here." You offer comfort without pressure. Presence without interrogation. You give her a handhold without turning it into a spotlight.

A lot of men think they're being punished during these moments. Like she's withholding connection on purpose, and your job is to figure out the riddle. But she's not punishing you — she's navigating her own internal mess while deciding whether she can trust you to handle it. And if every time she's messy, you either leave the room or try to logic her out of her feelings, you're answering that question very clearly. And not in your favor.

There's also the physiological reality. Yes, hormones are real. No, they're not an excuse. But they are a factor. If your wife is like most women, her body cycles through hormonal shifts every month that affect her mood, energy, focus, and stress levels — even if she doesn't talk about it. She might feel anxious for no clear reason. She might snap at something small and know it's irrational, but not be able to stop herself. And she'll probably try to keep it together for as long as possible, until something dumb — like the dishwasher being loaded wrong — pushes her over the edge. Then you're standing there, stunned, because you think you're being yelled at about plates, when really, you're standing in the fallout of five different stressors, four days of poor sleep, and an emotional backlog she hasn't had time to process.

You can't fix that. You shouldn't try to. What you *can* do is stop making it about you.

Instead of reacting with, "Geez, why are you being so sensitive?" you say, "You seem tense — want a break or a hand?" Instead of shutting down because her tone's off, you pause and ask yourself, *Is this about now, or is this something deeper that I can help anchor her through?*

You don't have to get it perfect. You just have to get involved. Not with commentary or analysis, but with care. With proximity. With calm.

Over time, she'll start to see you differently. Not as someone who gets everything right, but as someone who doesn't bolt when things get uncomfortable. That's a rare trait. And when she feels safe enough to bring you the real stuff — the messy, wordless, vulnerable moments — you'll realize that this isn't about moods. It's about trust. It's about building a marriage where she doesn't feel like she has to carry everything alone, even when she's not being easy to love.

None of this will show up on a marriage license. No one gives you a checklist for it. But it's the core of emotional partnership. And the more consistent you are, the fewer of those "I'm fine" landmines you'll have to navigate — not because they disappear, but because she'll know she doesn't have to hide behind them anymore.

That doesn't mean the weather always clears. But it does mean you learn how to keep the windows open without fear of being blown out of the house.

And at a certain point, you stop checking the radar and start noticing the signs yourself. Not to fix them. Just to be ready when the clouds come.

That's the work. That's the shift.

And it's where you start learning what it actually means to be someone's safe place.

3: Decorative Pillows and Hidden Landmines
(What She Cares About That You Don't Get Yet)

There's a moment in every new husband's life when he's standing in a room — maybe the living room, maybe the bedroom — and he looks around, confused, because somehow he has become surrounded by a growing colony of decorative objects he neither purchased nor understands.

Pillows that serve no purpose. Baskets that contain... smaller baskets. Towels you're not allowed to use. Frames with quotes you didn't approve, arranged in a gallery pattern that apparently took two hours and three mood boards to design.

And in this moment, as you stand there in your socks holding a remote, it hits you: this isn't your space anymore. This is *ours.* Which — if we're being honest — mostly means *hers.*

Now, to be clear: she probably doesn't care about *everything.* You're still allowed to have your favorite coffee mug. Maybe you get to keep your worn-out hoodie or the one kitchen knife you claim is better than all the others. But for the most part, you are now living in a space that reflects her sense of what "home" feels like — and her vision of "home" doesn't include your collection of lanyards from past beer festivals.

The problem isn't that she's decorating. It's that she cares so deeply about things you've never even *noticed.* Placement. Texture. Warmth. The energy of a space. How it feels to walk into a room and not be confronted by a tangled nest of charging cords or your crusty basketball shorts slung over the back of a dining chair.

This is where men get confused — not just because you don't share her priorities, but because you don't *see* them. You don't see the fingerprints on the mirror until she points them out. You don't notice the lumpy throw pillows unless they're physically in your way. You don't care about candles or diffusers or matching bookends. And if you're honest, you kind of resent how much she seems to care.

But here's what you're missing: this isn't about stuff. It's about security. Control. Sanity.

For her, the state of the home often mirrors the state of her mind. When things are chaotic outside, she craves order inside. When the world feels heavy, she creates light — with color, softness, beauty. That candle isn't just a scent; it's an act of self-regulation. The color-coded shelves aren't just for aesthetics; they're for clarity. That framed art print above the bed wasn't just a cute Etsy find — it was a way of planting a flag and saying, "This space matters to me."

You may not understand it, but you're living in it now. And you need to start treating her domestic instincts as part of who she is — not a quirk to tolerate, and definitely not something to tease.

This doesn't mean you have to pretend you love throw pillows. But it does mean you need to stop treating her preferences like optional background noise. Because when you act like the little things don't matter — like you don't care whether your shoes are left in the hallway or if you wiped down the counter or if the "good towels" are used to clean up dog vomit — what she hears is that *she* doesn't matter.

You think you're saying, *What's the big deal?*
She hears, *Your effort is invisible to me.*

The emotional labor of creating a home is mostly unseen. You don't notice when the hand soap gets refilled — you notice when it runs out. You don't appreciate that the junk drawer has been quietly reorganized — you just assume it always functioned. You didn't realize the silverware drawer used to be a mess because it was never a mess *while you lived there.*

That's how you end up stepping into one of these emotional sinkholes without warning. You toss a dirty sock on a just-made bed and she snaps. You leave the lights on in three rooms and she glares at you like you've personally declared war on her sanity. And in your head, you're thinking, *Wow, she's really making a big deal out of nothing.*

But it's not nothing. It's cumulative. It's a slow build of disrespect — not intentional, maybe, but consistent. She's trying to build a life with someone who keeps shrugging at the things she cares about most. She's asking you to participate in the shared space like an adult, not like a guy crashing on his girlfriend's couch until his band gets a record deal.

The irony here is that you probably think of yourself as "chill." You're not high-maintenance. You don't make a fuss. You don't need things to be perfect. Which you assume makes you easy to live with.

But from her perspective, "low-maintenance" can sometimes look a lot like *passive.* You're not helping make decisions. You're not noticing when things need care. You're not carrying the mental load of maintaining your shared life. You're just floating — and leaving her to do the rowing.

This doesn't mean you have to become a Pinterest-happy, eucalyptus-hanging, coasters-for-different-moods kind of guy. But it does mean you need to step into your space — your actual physical space — with some damn awareness.

If she just cleaned, don't explode into the living room with your backpack and your gym bag and your takeout containers and plop down like you're a wounded linebacker coming off the field. If she's trying to make a room feel peaceful, don't blare the game at full volume and toss your socks at the wall like it's your personal laundry contest. If she buys new pillows, you don't need to love them — but maybe don't immediately announce that they're "weirdly small" and "kind of itchy" before she's even taken the tags off.

None of this is about decor. It's about attention. Respect. Participation.

Because when you start showing that you *see* what she's building — not just with words, but with behavior — everything gets easier. She doesn't have to nag. She doesn't have to hover. She doesn't have to explain, again, why the good towels are for guests and not for mopping up spaghetti sauce.

She'll trust you more, not because you folded a blanket properly, but because she knows you understand why it matters to her. And that shift — from tolerating her preferences to respecting them — is what makes the difference between being her husband and just being her housemate with benefits.

That's the learning curve. You won't get it right every time. You'll use the wrong sponge or rearrange the pantry without permission and she'll act like you rewired her soul. But you'll get better. You'll ask questions. You'll notice things. You'll realize that love lives in the details — not the big dramatic gestures, but in the way you handle the everyday stuff that tells her, even without words, that her world matters to you.

The hidden landmines will still be there. They always are. But if you're willing to slow down and actually learn the terrain, you'll trip over fewer of them. And when you do, you'll know how to recover — not by defending yourself, but by listening, adjusting, and trying again.

Because that's how you build a home with someone. One compromise, one shared drawer, one pillow at a time.

4: "Helping" Is Not a Love Language

(Why She's Not Clapping Just Because You Took Out the Trash)

At some point in your married life — probably sooner rather than later — you're going to take out the trash and expect applause. Maybe not a literal standing ovation, but at least a "Thanks, babe" or a kiss or a validating nod that says, *Yes, you're a good man. You noticed a task, and you did it.*

What you might get instead is… nothing. Or worse, a flat look that says, *Do you want a prize?* You'll feel a flicker of indignation. After all, you didn't have to take out the trash. You did it to be helpful. Shouldn't that count for something?

This is where you discover that your understanding of "helping" — a concept you've been praised for since you were old enough to carry in a bag of groceries —

doesn't quite mean the same thing to your wife. In fact, the very idea of "helping" may be part of the problem.

Because what she hears when you say you "helped" is that the responsibility for the household is fundamentally hers, and you're offering assistance like a friendly neighbor. You're stepping into a job that isn't yours — doing it kindly, perhaps — but still seeing it as optional. Voluntary. Bonus work. Which means that in your eyes, the baseline standard is still her doing everything, and you doing something above and beyond.

That's not partnership. That's delegation. That's showing up to a group project and asking what you can do after she's already outlined the goals, divided the tasks, and started the PowerPoint.

It's not that she's ungrateful you took the trash out. It's that she's already exhausted from carrying all the things you don't see. Not just physical chores, but decisions. Planning. Anticipating needs. Managing time, meals, errands, appointments, emotional tone, and whether or not the guest towels are clean for her mother's visit. So when you announce you "helped," it feels less like a contribution and more like a reminder that she's still the one keeping the wheels turning while you drop in when it's convenient.

Now, none of this means you're lazy or entitled. In fact, you probably think you're doing more than most guys you know. You make the bed, you load the dishwasher, you even vacuum once in a while. You're trying. But trying without understanding the full context of what your wife is managing will only get you so far. She doesn't want a helper — she wants a partner who sees what needs doing and does it *without being asked.*

And if your instinct here is to say, "Well, just tell me what you want me to do," understand that this response — no matter how well-meaning — sounds to her like an admission that you expect to be managed. That you're waiting for a list. That the work isn't really yours until she assigns it. That she's still the one holding the mental clipboard and keeping track of what's been done, what hasn't, and who needs to do what next.

That's the mental load. It's the unpaid, unspoken job of noticing what needs to happen in a household, planning it, tracking it, remembering it, and executing it — or making sure someone else does. And the reason she seems irritated that you didn't fold the laundry the "right" way or left the wet towel on the bed isn't because she's controlling or picky. It's because she's tired of being the only one who notices and gives a damn.

The more you expect her to assign you tasks, the more you reinforce her role as the default parent, manager, or forewoman of your shared life. And that's what wears her down — not that you forgot to squeegee the shower, but that you never even considered whether the shower *needed* squeegeeing.

This dynamic becomes even more noticeable if and when kids enter the picture. If you think the mental load is heavy now, wait until you add school schedules, doctor visits, packing lunches, remembering whose turn it is to bring snacks to soccer, and fielding emotional meltdowns from multiple humans at once. At that point, "I helped with dinner" starts to sound a lot like "I watered one plant while you mowed the entire yard."

But even if you're not there yet — even if it's just the two of you — the imbalance creeps in quietly. When she starts anticipating needs and solving problems before you even notice them, you get used to not having to think about it. She takes care of the birthday gifts. She plans the trip. She buys the laundry detergent before it runs out. She arranges dinner with your parents and remembers what your mom doesn't like to eat. You feel supported, even lucky. She feels alone in the responsibility.

And when she eventually snaps — not because of one thing, but because of the slow buildup of it all — you feel blindsided. You were trying. You were doing your part. You don't understand where all the resentment came from.

It came from managing you. From being the only one who had a running list in her head while you kept asking what needed to be done next.

If you want to fix this — really fix it — you have to start noticing. And then you have to start *owning.* You look around and ask, "What needs doing in this house that I never think about?" You take full ownership of something and commit to running it completely — laundry, meals, budgeting, pet care, whatever. You make the decisions. You track the supplies. You anticipate the needs. You don't wait to be told, and you don't expect gold stars when you do it.

And no, this doesn't mean you'll always do it "her way." That's fine. She can adjust to different methods. What she can't adjust to is the feeling that she's stuck carrying all the logistics forever while you float around like a consultant who steps in occasionally with good intentions and the emotional self-awareness of a distracted intern.

You'll screw up. She will too. That's not the point. The point is whether you're paying attention — not just to what's being done, but to *who's doing the thinking* behind the scenes. Because that's where the fatigue builds. And that's what turns a woman from soft to sharp, from generous to guarded, from trusting to transactional.

If you want her to feel safe, seen, and equal in this partnership, she needs to believe that the labor of building a life together doesn't fall mostly on her shoulders. She needs to see you show up before she burns out — not after.

That doesn't come from big gestures. It comes from watching her do the dishes while you sit on your phone, realizing, *I should be helping,* and then not just helping — but realizing the problem was that you needed to *notice* in the first place.

5: Sleeping with the Enemy

(Why Sharing a Bed Is a Full-Contact Sport)

When you imagined married life, you probably included a shared bed in that picture — soft lighting, maybe a candle flickering on the dresser, the two of you tangled together under a neatly arranged duvet. You imagined comfort. Closeness. Intimacy.

What you got instead is a war zone.

She kicks. You snore. She has nine pillows. You use one that smells like your scalp and has existed since high school. She wants a soft blanket cocoon with a weighted topper and precisely folded corners. You sleep like a Labrador — spread out, belly up, mouth open, radiating heat like a busted radiator.

The marriage bed is not a peaceful place. It is not a sanctuary of romantic stillness. It is, at best, a live negotiation. At worst, it's a nightly battle for real estate, air flow, and blanket access.

You may think, *It's just sleep. Why does it matter so much?* Because sleep isn't just sleep. It's recovery. It's rhythm. It's the only time in your day when you stop performing — and if you're making her miserable in that state, it's going to bleed into every waking hour.

Let's start with the layout. You probably assumed your queen-sized bed would be plenty. It's not. A queen bed is large enough for one adult and one cat. Maybe a small dog. But two fully grown humans, one of whom flails in REM and the other of whom clutches a body pillow like it's an emotional flotation device? Not a chance. What looks generous on paper feels, in practice, like sleeping on a twin with aspirations.

You'll begin to notice things — patterns. Her side will always be neatly tucked, and yours will look like a drunken otter attempted to make a nest. She'll adjust her pillow with military precision, smoothing the pillowcase and re-centering the decorative sham. You will punch your pillow once and throw your arm across your eyes like a man betrayed. She turns off the light. You turn on your phone. She tries to drift. You decide this is the perfect moment to catch up on loud TikToks you claim are "educational."

Then the temperature battle begins. She is cold. Always. Even in summer. Even under three blankets. Her feet, somehow, radiate glacier-level frost through layers of socks and sheets. You, meanwhile, produce body heat like a nuclear reactor. She inches closer for warmth. You shift away to avoid the sensation of being smothered by a hot, damp human fog. The thermostat becomes a symbol of marital compromise — or failure. She wants it at 74. You want it at 68. You end up at 71, and neither of you is happy.

The snoring, though — that's the real villain. You won't believe you snore. You may even deny it. Then one night, she records you. And you hear it — a deep, guttural chain saw of nasal obstruction, followed by a sudden choking gasp that sounds like a dying animal. You try to laugh. She does not. You promise to try nasal strips. You forget. She brings them up again, less gently this time. You end up having a serious conversation about sleep apnea while brushing your teeth.

There's also movement. You sprawl. You flip. You adjust and toss and let your knee wander to wherever gravity sends it. She, in contrast, finds a comfortable position and clings to it like a disciplined yogi. You drift off like a dog circling its spot, adjusting and grumbling and nudging the blanket six times before settling. She stares at the ceiling, wide awake, wondering why you only get still after she's hit full REM and has just begun dreaming about a cabin in the woods where no one snores.

It's not just the physical chaos. There are politics, too. Blanket equity is a real issue. You will wake up clinging to a strip of comforter no wider than a tie, while she is swaddled in enough fabric to upholster a loveseat. She won't know how it happened. You will insist she's hoarding. The passive-aggressive tugs begin. If you're lucky, you'll both laugh. If not, the silent Cold War continues until someone threatens to buy a second blanket.

And there's the occasional assault. The way she elbows you when you snore. The way you fling your leg over her thigh in what you think is a loving gesture but what she experiences as a 3 a.m. hamstring cramp. You'll both pretend you sleep peacefully through the night. Neither of you does. Sleep becomes a game of compromise, survival, and ignoring the bruises you wake up with.

But the real challenge is emotional. Because sleep isn't just about physical proximity — it's about vulnerability. It's the one time when both of you are completely unguarded. And when something goes wrong — when she can't sleep because you're tossing, when you're sweating because she's draped over you like a comfort koala, when the bed feels like a crime scene of poor circulation and mutual resentment — it begins to affect how you see each other.

You don't say it. But you both feel it. You tiptoe around the subject in the morning. "Did you sleep okay?" "Yeah, not really." "Same." But what you're not saying is, *This setup isn't working. And it's making me like you less at night.*

The couples who last aren't the ones who get it perfect. They're the ones who adapt. Some sleep with separate blankets. Some sleep in separate beds a few nights a week and call it strategic, not shameful. Some wear earplugs, some use white noise machines, some invest in mattress toppers thick enough to smother a conflict. Some try melatonin and wind-down routines and soft lighting and breathing apps. Others just sigh and learn to accept that sleeping next to another adult human is never going to be like the movies.

You'll find what works. But not without acknowledging that something *isn't* working. And if you want sleep to be a source of closeness instead of quiet contempt, you're going to have to start talking about it.

That means admitting your habits. Asking about hers. Acknowledging that your comfort may sometimes mean her discomfort, and that the solution isn't to pretend it's all fine — it's to find the in-between. The temperature setting that works. The compromise on snoring. The real discussion about whether a king bed might save your marriage before year two.

Because yes, sleep matters. It doesn't seem romantic. It doesn't look like the stuff of emotional connection. But the truth is, how you rest next to someone is often the best indicator of how you live next to them.

The bed is where everything begins and ends. If that place becomes a source of tension, it leaks into the rest of your day. You snap more. You resent more. You find yourself quietly rooting against each other in the battle of comfort and control.

But when you get it right — or at least get closer to right — things change. She relaxes. You relax. Sleep becomes a refuge again. Not a performance. Not a competition. Just two people, side by side, figuring out how to share space in the dark, and still want to be close when the light comes back on.

6: Emotions for Dummies

Why She Thinks You're Emotionally Distant — and What You're Missing

At some point in your early months of marriage, you're going to notice something strange. It may happen during an argument, or while you're watching TV, or right after she's shared something vulnerable and you've said nothing back. You'll realize you've been mentally filing away your feelings like a poorly run DMV — and that the system is starting to break down.

You'll start to see how often you default to silence, or avoidance, or flat denial. She'll ask, "What's going on with you?" and you'll say, "Nothing." She'll ask how you're feeling, and you'll say, "I don't know." She'll ask what's wrong, and you'll say, "I'm fine," even though your face is saying *I'm trying not to throw a chair through the wall right now.* You'll do this not to be difficult, not because you enjoy being cryptic — but because you don't know how to put the experience of your emotions into words. You were never taught.

Women, on the other hand, are often trained from a young age to read feelings — not just their own, but everyone else's. They're expected to mediate, reflect, express, and intuit. They've been handed vocabulary for emotion, and more importantly, permission to use it. You were handed a towel and told to walk it off.

That means she's showing up to conversations with fluency in a language you barely know how to pronounce. When she says she feels overwhelmed, anxious, unappreciated, or emotionally isolated, she means exactly that. When you say "I'm fine," she hears emotional cowardice. Or worse, a brush-off.

This is where the frustration begins. She's not mad that you don't know what you're feeling. She's mad that you don't even seem interested in trying to figure it out. You act like emotions are optional. You treat them like software you didn't install, so you guess you'll just get by without it. But the longer you defer this work, the more you become impossible to connect with.

Eventually, she starts filling in the blanks for you. If you don't name what's wrong, she'll guess. She'll interpret silence as withdrawal. She'll mistake your disconnection for disinterest. And since you're still not saying anything — because you're not sure how — you can't correct her. Now you're both annoyed, neither of you knows exactly why, and any chance at resolution is buried under a pile of unsaid things.

Let's get one thing straight. Emotions aren't "feminine." They're not irrational. They're not weak. They are data — just like everything else you rely on to make decisions. And if you're pretending you don't have them, or that they don't matter, you're not being strong. You're being unavailable.

That's not what she signed up for.

You may think you're keeping the peace by staying quiet when you're upset. You may tell yourself you're being respectful by not starting a fight. But from her perspective, your silence is not neutral — it's unsettling. It feels like you're emotionally MIA. Like you'd rather bite your tongue into bloody strips than risk saying something honest and uncomfortable. And while you might think that's a form of restraint, what she experiences is a form of absence.

You don't have to give a TED Talk about your feelings. But you do need to give her *something.*

Try this: instead of saying "I'm fine," say, "I'm not sure what I'm feeling right now, but I know something's off." Instead of shutting down after a hard day, say, "Can we talk in a bit? I'm sorting out some stuff in my head." If you feel angry and you don't know why, say that. You don't have to arrive at the perfect emotional summary — but you do have to let her into the process.

Because the truth is, she's not expecting you to have all the answers. She's just expecting you to try. To be honest about where you are emotionally, even if where you are is *lost*.

Here's a hard truth: if you refuse to do this work — if you keep showing up emotionally mute and expecting her to drag it out of you — she will eventually stop asking. Not because she's over it, but because she's tired. Because she's done trying to pull your feelings out of you like a dentist extracting molars. And once she gives up trying to know you emotionally, you'll start to feel that distance everywhere — in the bedroom, in the way she talks to you, in how often she shares her own heart. She won't be withholding on purpose. She's just matching your energy. That's what people do when they realize intimacy isn't being reciprocated.

Of course, all of this assumes you actually *want* to be known — which, deep down, you probably do. But wanting it isn't enough. You have to learn how to show up emotionally in real time. That means slowing down and asking yourself what you're actually feeling, instead of reacting out of habit. It means naming frustration instead of masking it with sarcasm. It means identifying fear instead of snapping about logistics. And yes, it means getting it wrong sometimes — but showing her that you're willing to get in the ring anyway.

That vulnerability might feel awkward at first. Forced. Even weak. But it's not. In fact, in her eyes, it's one of the most attractive things you can do — not just because it helps her feel closer to you, but because it signals something bigger: that you trust her with your inner world. That you're brave enough to be seen without armor.

What matters is not the precision of your language, but the effort behind it. The willingness to stretch past your comfort zone, to try a sentence that might not come out perfectly, to stay in the room when things feel emotionally messy instead of retreating into numbness or distraction. That effort lands harder than you think. It shows her that you're not just present in body, but present in mind and heart.

And if she's doing this work already — if she's showing up emotionally, naming her needs, expressing her highs and lows with honesty and courage — then you don't just owe her your love. You owe her your growth. You owe her the effort of learning to speak your own heart in a way that doesn't make her carry both sides of every hard conversation.

If you never do this — if you stay silent, if you keep zoning out, if you treat emotional conversations like quicksand you must avoid — she'll eventually accept the fact that you're just not capable of going there. And once she believes that, she will adjust her expectations permanently. Not because she doesn't care, but because she's done being disappointed.

You don't want that. You don't want a marriage where everything feels fine on paper but emotionally hollow in practice. You don't want a relationship where you sleep in the same bed but feel like strangers when you try to talk about anything real.

You want to be understood. But you can't be understood if you don't speak. You want connection. But you can't get connection by hiding. You want respect. But you have to earn it by being brave enough to share the parts of yourself that don't come naturally.

No one expects perfection. But if you want to be loved deeply, you have to learn how to be seen — and that only happens when you're willing to bring something real to the surface and leave it there long enough for her to reach for it. Not as a test, and not as a performance. Just as truth. Hers and yours, side by side, in the same room, at the same emotional altitude. That's where the real connection begins — and where it's sustained.

7: Man Flu and Other Life-Threatening Non-Emergencies

(Why She Stops Caring When You Act Like You're Dying of a Sore Throat)

At some point in your marriage — possibly the first fall flu season — you will get sick. Not deathbed sick. Not ER sick. But sick enough to make noises. Sniffling, coughing, throat-clearing, and the kind of dramatic exhaling normally reserved for war movies and childbirth. You will burrow under a blanket. You will ask if she thinks you have a fever. You will hold your head like Hamlet holding Yorick's skull and declare, "I think I might be coming down with something."

And she will blink. Maybe offer you tea. Maybe just say, "Okay." But what she will *not* do is respond with the level of alarm and sympathy you expect. You'll notice this, and it will confuse you.

That confusion is what we're here to clear up.

Because what's happening isn't about cold medicine. It's about contrast. It's about what she does when *she* is sick — and what you do when *you* are.

Let's walk through the comparison.

When she has a headache, she takes something and keeps going. When she has cramps, she still goes to work. When she has a sinus infection, she reschedules a dentist appointment, buys groceries, and still remembers your nephew's birthday. You probably didn't even know she was sick until day four, when she finally mentions it in passing while still making dinner.

When you have a mild cough, you melt.

You make a nest on the couch. You begin monitoring your temperature with the diligence of a NASA flight technician. You ask questions like, "Do you think this is bronchitis or just allergies?" even though it's clearly just allergies. You groan when you stand up. You mention it at least four times per hour, even if nothing has changed.

She notices.

And no, she doesn't think you're weak. What she thinks is that you've never had to build the habit of functioning through discomfort. That you were raised — directly or indirectly — to believe that when men are sick, the world slows down around them. That their

42

partners step in. That their needs come first, even if it's just the common cold.

You may not think you're expecting special treatment. But she's lived with you long enough to see that when you're even slightly under the weather, you begin to act like a tragic figure from a Victorian novel. You shuffle. You sigh. You drape yourself over furniture like your bones are made of regret. You describe your symptoms in vivid, theatrical terms. "It feels like there's a weight on my chest," you say, as if you've just emerged from a coal mine.

She is not impressed.

Because here's what she knows — and what you probably haven't thought about: illness, for her, is rarely a pause button. It's an inconvenience. One more thing to manage while everything else continues. She has to plan around it. She has to absorb the hit. There's no couch-nesting fantasy. There's only logistics: how to get through the week without collapsing.

So when you act like your sore throat has upended your entire identity, she doesn't feel moved. She feels insulted. Not because you're sick, but because your default setting seems to be: "I need help," while hers has always been: "Figure it out."

This doesn't mean you're not allowed to feel bad. Or to need comfort. But it *does* mean that how you carry yourself when you're sick sends a bigger message than you think. It tells her how you handle discomfort. It tells her whether you're someone who expects to be rescued. And it tells her whether you understand the difference between real need and performative helplessness.

And if you really want to light a fire under her resentment, try this: compare your cold to something she's experienced and suggest yours is worse. Say, "I think this is worse than when you had that root canal." Say it casually, while she's folding laundry you've left sitting out for two days. See how fast her eyes narrow.

There's a reason the term "man flu" exists. It's not just a joke. It's a shorthand for a pattern women have experienced so often it no longer surprises them. The way men often fold in the face of minor illness, and expect full-service care, while women are expected to gut it out and still make it to that baby shower with a smile on their face.

You can break this pattern. It's not complicated. The next time you feel off — like you might be getting sick — pause before making it a household-wide event. Take care of yourself. Drink water. Cancel something if you need to. But don't act like the universe owes you emotional backup for every sniffle.

More importantly, think about how you respond when *she's* not feeling well. Are you attentive without needing to be asked? Do you offer to take something off her plate — not as a big favor, but as a basic sign of support? Or do you treat her illness like background noise, assuming she'll push through because that's what she always does?

If the answer is the latter, then it's no wonder she's short on compassion when the roles are reversed. She's learned, from experience, that she has to be her own nurse, scheduler, and cheerleader. So when you expect her to drop everything and dote on you, it doesn't feel endearing. It feels like hypocrisy.

There's nothing wrong with needing care. She wants to care for you — but not when the energy imbalance is so stark that it feels like another job. You want her sympathy? Then meet her standard. Show that you can handle discomfort with some grit. That you can ask for support without turning into a patient. That you're capable of recognizing when it's time to push through, and when it's okay to rest — *without* making it everyone's problem.

Illness isn't just about health. It's a window into how you handle vulnerability, and whether you've developed the skill of staying grounded when your body throws a curveball. She's watching. Not to judge, but to gauge — how much she'll be expected to carry if something ever really *does* go wrong. And whether you're someone who can be leaned on, not just looked after.

That's what she wants to see. Not toughness for its own sake, but emotional maturity. The ability to be human — sick, tired, off your game — without outsourcing the entire experience to the nearest woman.

And if you can learn to manage those small illnesses with humility and self-awareness? She'll notice that too. She may even start showing more tenderness, because now she sees you taking responsibility — not just for your cold, but for the way you inhabit your own body and ask for care like an adult, not a sitcom caricature.

The next time you're sick, don't reach for the drama. Reach for the medicine. Take a nap. Skip the narration. Then go thank her for that soup you didn't ask her to make. It'll land harder than any dramatic sneeze.

8: The Lost Art of Listening
(Why She Thinks You Don't Hear Her — Even When You're Nodding)

Somewhere in your first year of marriage — maybe after a long day, maybe in the middle of a minor disagreement, maybe while she's telling you about something that happened at work — you'll nod while she talks. You'll say "yeah," or "totally," or maybe even "that sucks." And you'll think, *I'm doing a good job here. I'm listening. I'm being present.*

But she won't feel heard.

You'll know that when she either says it out loud — "Are you even listening?" — or lets it show through the kind of frosty silence that doesn't melt easily. And you'll be confused. You were there. You didn't interrupt. You even remembered to put your phone down this time. Why does she seem frustrated?

Because to her, you weren't really *listening*. You were just physically present while she talked.

There's a difference, and she knows it — probably better than you do. Because women are trained, from an early age, to sense whether someone is emotionally engaged. To read micro-reactions, body language, timing, tone, pauses. Listening is not just auditory for her. It's relational. She knows when someone is leaning in with curiosity, and when someone is leaning back with quiet impatience.

Men, on the other hand, are trained to listen just enough to know when it's their turn to speak. To scan for key facts, assess the point, and respond only when there's something to fix or clarify. Listening, for most men, is transactional. For most women, it's connective.

This is why you keep having conversations where she opens up and you think it went fine — only to find out later that she walked away feeling emotionally dismissed. It's not that you didn't care. It's that you didn't *show* that you cared in a way that landed for her.

Let's say she comes home from work and starts venting about a team meeting. She says something like, "I don't know why they keep asking for feedback and then ignoring it. I'm tired of speaking up if no one's listening." You respond, "Yeah, that's how offices are." To you, that's an agreement — a gesture of solidarity. But to her, it feels like you just minimized the entire experience. Like you waved it away as something normal and not worth discussing.

What she wanted wasn't your solution. Or even your opinion. What she wanted was your attention. She wanted to feel like you were tracking with her, that you were taking in the details, that you could reflect some of the frustration she was feeling. Not mirror it. Not fix it. Just *meet her there* for a moment.

It's maddening for women — truly maddening — to have to explain why being heard matters. Because for many of them, being heard has always been optional in the lives of the men around them. Fathers who tuned out. Bosses who bulldozed. Boyfriends who nodded while watching TV. Teachers who cut them off mid-sentence. The bar is low. But it's still rarely met.

So when she chooses to open up to you, and you offer her the same kind of casual, half-engaged response she's gotten her whole life, it hits harder than you realize. It reinforces the idea that even in her most intimate relationship, she still has to fight to be understood.

Over time, this compounds. The first few times, she'll let it slide. But as it builds, she'll start doing something that will probably confuse you — she'll stop talking. Not completely. Not all at once. But gradually, she'll begin sharing less. You'll feel like things are "easier" between you. Less emotional. Less tense.

They're not easier. She's just retreating.

When a woman stops trying to be heard, it's not peace. It's surrender. And that emotional distance — that shift from trust to guardedness — is one of the slowest, saddest erosions that can happen inside a marriage. You may not even see it happening until one day she says something like, "I don't feel like we talk anymore," or worse, "I don't feel close to you."

And you'll be floored. Because to you, nothing seemed wrong. But the intimacy that listening provides had been quietly leaking out of the relationship for months — and you didn't even know it was happening.

It's not all bad news, though. This is a skill. You can learn it. And when you do, it changes the whole dynamic.

Start with this: **listen without assuming a job assignment is coming.** Don't treat her words like a problem to solve. She's not always asking for action. Sometimes she just wants a witness.

Second, **listen without waiting to be right.** Especially during an argument. If she says, "You made me feel like I didn't matter," don't immediately jump to defend yourself. Don't say, "That's not what I meant," or "You're being too sensitive." Instead, ask her to explain more. Say, "I didn't realize that's how it came across — what part made you feel that way?" Not because you're accepting blame, but because you care enough to *understand.*

Third, **listen like it matters.** Because it does. If she says something emotional and you barely look up from your phone, that registers as disinterest. Not just in what she's saying, but in *her.* And once that seed is planted — that you're not emotionally invested — it takes a lot of effort to dig it out.

You don't need to remember every word. But you do need to remember what matters. If she says her boss has been stressing her out, and you check in about it two days later, it tells her you were paying attention. That you're not just a passenger in the conversation — you're in the car with her. You're following the route. That small follow-up lands more than any big romantic gesture you could pull off.

Good listening also means **creating space for her to speak freely.** That means no mocking her tone, no mimicking her words, no sighing or checking your watch mid-conversation. You think you're being subtle when you do that? You're not. She notices. And it tells her that her feelings are making you uncomfortable — which means she'll start editing herself, or cutting her thoughts short, or deciding that it's just not worth the hassle to explain something if it's going to be met with flippant resistance.

And the stakes are not just emotional. When women feel heard in their relationship, they are more affectionate. More trusting. More sexually open. More forgiving. More invested in solving problems together. Not because you "earned points," but because they feel like they're *in a relationship with someone who actually knows them.*

On the flip side, when women feel *unheard,* they become cold. Dismissive. Cynical. They hold grudges longer. They interpret your actions less generously. They stop believing in your capacity to grow. Not because they're trying to punish you, but because they've stopped believing that you actually care about their internal world. And once they stop believing that, they stop showing you that world altogether.

You don't need to become a poet. You don't need to start reading self-help books or asking "how does that make you feel" in your best therapy voice. You just need to stop faking it. You need to decide, deliberately, that when she's speaking — especially about something real — you're going to show up with your full attention, and not just out of obligation.

That means putting the phone down. Turning the TV off. Looking at her face. Responding to what she's *actually* saying, not what you assumed she meant. Following up later. Checking back in.

It's not complicated. But it does require effort. And if it's hard for you to put that effort in, ask yourself why. Ask yourself what you think listening is "supposed to be." Because if your definition of listening still centers around waiting for your turn to talk or deciding whether or not you agree, you've missed the point completely.

She doesn't need an echo. She needs an anchor. Someone who can sit with her feelings without rushing them, or reframing them, or editing them down to something more comfortable. If you can do that — if you can develop the muscle of sitting with what she's actually saying, even when it's awkward or emotional or unclear — she will trust you with bigger things. Things she hasn't told anyone. Things that *matter* to her on a deep, cellular level.

And if you don't? She'll still talk. But eventually, she won't be talking to you.

That's not a threat. That's gravity. Conversations are like water. They flow where they're received. Your job isn't to be the smartest guy in the room — it's to be the one who listens well enough that she doesn't have to leave the room to feel understood.

9: Decorating Delusions

Why She Hates Your Flag, Your Recliner, and Your Taste in Lamps

You're going to come home one day and realize your apartment — or your shared starter home, or your post-honeymoon rental — doesn't look like your space anymore. At first, it'll be small. A decorative tray where your keys used to land. A wall mirror you're pretty sure wasn't there last week. A pillow with tassels that seems to serve no practical purpose but which now occupies the center of the bed like a smug decorative overlord.

You'll make a joke about it. Something harmless, like, "We really needed another candle, huh?" She'll smile, maybe. Or maybe she'll give you a look that says, *You think I don't notice when you mock things you don't understand?*

Because here's the thing: you don't understand. Not yet. And the sooner you realize that decorating isn't just about aesthetics to her — it's about identity, security, and psychological grounding — the sooner you'll stop making sarcastic comments that only confirm how much you're missing the point.

Men and women often approach shared spaces differently. For many men, especially if you lived alone for a while, decorating a home was more or less a mix of survival, minimalism, and personal nostalgia. A couch, a TV, a piece of sports memorabilia. Maybe a flag. A poster from college you keep meaning to frame. A coffee table that doubles as footrest, dinner tray, and laundry sorter. Done.

She walks in, sees that setup, and her whole body tenses. It's not about disliking your stuff — it's about what it represents. It says, "This is my space. You can live in it, but it's been shaped around what makes *me* comfortable." That's not inviting. That's territorial.

She wants more than furniture that works. She wants warmth. She wants intention. She wants the place you both live to feel like somewhere she'd choose to be, not where she's been absorbed into a bachelor habitat that survived the marriage license.

And yes — she will begin changing things. Pillows, rugs, curtains, lighting, storage solutions that double as decor. The TV might move. The desk might rotate. The walls will develop opinions. And your impulse will be to resist. To defend the existing setup, even if you never gave it much thought before. You'll take it personally.

Like your identity is being erased by a can of eggshell paint.

But what she's trying to do — what she's often forced to do — is *build a shared space out of a man's leftovers.* She didn't inherit a blank canvas. She inherited your laundry chair, your ugly lamp, your complete indifference to lighting temperature, and your deeply held belief that hanging a flag counts as interior design.

Let's talk about the flag. Or the neon beer sign. Or the mounted jersey. Whatever your version is. You probably thought it was cool. Nostalgic. A tribute to your roots. And she's not trying to erase your history. She's trying to build a future that doesn't look like a dorm room.

You'll argue, of course. Or at least grumble. You'll ask why every blanket has to have a texture. Why there are three decorative pumpkins in the bathroom. Why one throw pillow is fine but five is a war crime. And her answers might not satisfy you, because they won't be about logic. They'll be about *feeling.*

That's what most men miss about how women decorate: it's not just visual. It's emotional. The goal isn't symmetry. It's serenity. It's walking into a room and exhaling. Not because everything is practical, but because everything is *intentional.*

And if you really want to strike a nerve, mock that intention. Treat her design choices like indulgences. Pretend the room just "became like this" without her effort. Say something offhanded like, "This looks like something my mom would've done," and watch how fast she shuts down.

Because what you're dismissing isn't just a pillow or a shelf arrangement. It's the hours she spent imagining what your life together could look like. The thought she gave to what colors would soften the space. The time she took to create something that didn't just feel like hers, but felt like *yours.* Something welcoming. Reflective. Peaceful.

This isn't about making everything her way. You're allowed to have opinions. But there's a difference between *having taste* and *being territorial.* When you reject her changes without offering real alternatives — or worse, without showing that you care at all — you're saying, "Your vision doesn't belong here." And in her mind, if her vision doesn't belong, maybe *she* doesn't either.

That might sound dramatic. But remember: women are often taught that their value lies in their ability to create comfort for others. When you shrug at that effort, or worse, roll your eyes at it, it feels like a rejection not just of her taste — but of her *offering.*

So what can you do instead?

Start by participating. Not controlling. Participating. Ask questions. Offer to help hang the shelves — without making it sound like a favor. Ask why she picked that print instead of joking about it. Don't roll your eyes when she lays out swatches. Don't call everything "decorative nonsense." Learn a few basic terms like "warm lighting" or "accent color" so she doesn't feel like she's decorating *around* you, like an inconvenient piece of furniture.

And maybe — just maybe — care a little. Not in the way that means you suddenly love scented candles and seasonal throw blankets. But in the way that means you see what she's doing and treat it like part of the real work of building a life. Because it is.

Your home is not a warehouse. It's not a default zone until something more important comes along. It's where you eat, sleep, argue, make up, raise kids (if you have them), and live out the tiny, forgettable, sacred routines that build a marriage. If it feels sterile, neglected, or one-sided, that shows up in every other part of the relationship. The house becomes another reminder of imbalance — another space where she shows up more than you do.

You'll still want your chair. Your ugly lamp. Your sacred hoodie corner. And fine — keep them. You deserve comfort, too. But when she tries to shift the space into something that reflects both of you, don't be the guy who digs in his heels because he thinks compromise means surrender.

Instead, be the guy who shows up with a hammer when she wants to hang floating shelves. Who surprises her by suggesting a new rug. Who doesn't always "get it," but stays curious enough to engage. That's the guy she wants to build a home with. Not the one who sulks because the recliner got moved three feet to the left.

It's not about the objects. It's about the atmosphere. It's about what it feels like to come home and exhale, together. And the more she sees you care about creating that with her, the less she'll feel like she has to decorate around your resistance — and the more she'll start to believe that this place, whatever it becomes, actually belongs to both of you.

10: Financial Foreplay

(Why She Thinks "We're Fine" Is Not a Budget — and She's Right)

You're going to think money talk is boring. Or stressful. Or unnecessary. That's normal. Most men don't get excited about spreadsheets unless there's a fantasy football angle. But at some point in your marriage — and probably sooner than you'd prefer — she's going to bring it up. Not in a combative way. Not necessarily because there's a crisis. But because she's scanning the future, and what she sees is a black box labeled *"You said we're fine."*

That phrase — "we're fine" — might be your favorite financial go-to. It's easy, casual, and non-committal. It suggests everything is under control without actually proving anything. It also gives her nothing to build from. Because unless she sees the math, knows the numbers, understands the flow, and has some sense of who's steering the financial ship — she doesn't believe you.

Not because she's suspicious. Because she's responsible.

She's not trying to micro-manage. She's trying to co-manage. And what you think of as "chill" — that laid-back, trust-me energy you pride yourself on — comes across to her as evasive. Immature. Potentially dangerous.

Let's talk about that disconnect.

You may see money as simple: pay the bills, keep food in the fridge, maybe save a little. If the lights are on and you're not overdrafting, then what's the problem?

She sees money as structural. It underpins your choices, your priorities, your stability, your values. When she asks about savings, it's not because she's obsessed with hoarding cash — it's because she's trying to sleep better at night knowing that one small emergency won't send your entire life into chaos.

And when you wave her off, deflect, or change the subject, she hears, *You're on your own if something goes wrong.*

Now, you might not *mean* that. You might fully intend to be there, to support her, to figure things out as they come. But that's not a plan. That's not leadership. That's gambling.

One of the most overlooked aspects of early marriage is how different financial personalities crash into each other. She may be a saver. You may be a spender. Or vice versa. She might be a detailed planner who knows the interest rate on every card and when the car insurance is due. You might feel confident as long as there's a positive balance in the checking account and you haven't bounced a payment this month.

The problem isn't your differences. The problem is when those differences go unacknowledged. When you each keep operating in your own lane without building a shared road map, your money habits become a constant undercurrent of low-grade friction.

You'll feel like she's "always stressing" about money. She'll feel like you never take it seriously. You'll want to buy something and feel judged. She'll ask about expenses and feel stonewalled. Eventually, every trip to Target or unplanned charge on the statement becomes a trigger for something bigger: mistrust.

What she wants — and may not have words for — is *financial intimacy.* Not just transparency. Connection. Confidence that you're both looking at the same future and actively making decisions to build it.

You might think the best way to avoid arguments is to keep things separate. "My money, her money." Or "I'll handle this, you handle that." That can work, but only if both people are equally informed, involved, and empowered. If your version of "separate finances" really just means "you don't get to ask questions," you're not building independence. You're building resentment.

And there are clues. If she gets quiet every time you casually drop $300 on a new hobby, she doesn't think you're irresponsible. She thinks you're inaccessible. That money is off-limits as a topic unless she wants to be seen as "nagging." So she stops bringing it up. But she doesn't stop worrying.

Or maybe she *is* a little controlling about spending. Maybe she needs more updates than you think are necessary. Before you label her high-maintenance, ask yourself where that's coming from. Is she trying to micromanage you, or is she reacting to a history where she felt unsupported? Is she carrying financial trauma from childhood? From a previous relationship? Or is she just tired of always being the one who knows when the bills are due?

And yes, there's another layer here — one men often miss. For many women, money isn't just about bills and savings. It's about power. Security. The ability to make decisions, to protect herself if things go wrong, to not be trapped. Even if she trusts you completely, she still needs to *see* that the foundation is solid. Not just hear it. See it. In statements, in habits, in behaviors.

That's why "we're fine" doesn't land. Because unless you've both sat down, looked at the numbers, discussed goals, and agreed on what "fine" means, the phrase is meaningless. It's like saying "we're probably not lost" while driving around a foreign country with the gas light on.

Start with the basics. What's the monthly total coming in, and what's going out? Are you saving anything? What's your debt load? What's your plan for the next year, or five? What happens if someone loses a job, or gets hurt, or wants to go back to school, or you suddenly need $5,000 for a car repair or a cross-country flight for a family emergency?

If you don't know, that's okay. You don't need to have all the answers. But you do need to start asking questions. And you need to bring her into that process — not as your financial babysitter, but as your co-pilot.

And when she brings concerns to the table, don't get defensive. If she says, "We need to talk about our budget," don't roll your eyes or make a joke about how she's turning into her mom. Sit down. Pull up the numbers. Treat it like a partnership, not a surprise audit.

Because when she sees you lean into those conversations — not just once, but consistently — she relaxes. Not because you suddenly turned into a financial advisor, but because you showed up. You proved that you're paying attention. That you're in this with her, fully, not just emotionally but operationally. That you take the stability of your shared life seriously enough to actually look at the damn numbers.

And yes, it can be boring. Or uncomfortable. But so is arguing about money every month because nobody ever set expectations. So is losing sleep wondering if the other person actually knows what things cost. So is fighting over impulse purchases or credit card debt or whether one of you is "allowed" to order takeout after a long week.

Financial foreplay isn't sexy because of the money. It's sexy because of what it communicates. I see you. I plan with you. I respect the stress you carry. I want to lead with you — not away from you, not around you, but next to you.

That's what turns budgets into trust. That's what makes her feel not just protected, but *in partnership.* And that's when the relationship stops feeling like a tug-of-war over who's spending what — and starts feeling like you're building something big together. Something with room for both of your goals, and a foundation strong enough to hold the life you're trying to create.

11: The Good Fight

(Why She's Not "Just Being Emotional" — and You're Not "Just Being Logical")

If you're like most men, you walk into conflict assuming you're being rational. Calm. Clear-headed. You might not say it out loud, but part of you believes you're the steady one. The facts guy. The voice of reason. Meanwhile, she's getting upset, raising her voice, spiraling into past grievances, "making everything about feelings."

From your vantage point, you're holding the line. She's overreacting.

From hers, you're dodging, dismissing, and — worst of all — refusing to actually participate.

Welcome to one of the most consistent breakdowns in modern relationships: *the myth of male logic versus female emotion.* It's a trap. And it keeps otherwise good couples stuck in the same frustrating cycle — where one partner feels attacked and the other feels abandoned.

Let's start with the obvious: conflict isn't the problem. Healthy couples fight. In fact, couples who never fight usually aren't communicating — they're avoiding. What matters isn't *if* you fight. It's how you fight. What the fight reveals. What gets said, what gets heard, and what gets left festering under the surface after the conversation is supposedly over.

When your wife gets upset — really upset — it's almost never because of just one thing. It's not that you didn't load the dishwasher. It's not that you forgot to text back. It's that those things stack up over time, and then one day, she trips on your shoes in the hallway and suddenly it's not about the shoes. It's about whether you're actually paying attention to your shared life — or just living in it like a long-term guest.

You, meanwhile, didn't see any of this coming. You thought things were fine. So when she starts venting, you think she's exaggerating. You don't remember doing half the things she's describing. You're annoyed that she's bringing up something from three weeks ago. And you're definitely not prepared for the tears — because now, instead of solving a problem, you're trying to manage a meltdown.

That's how you see it, anyway. She sees it differently.

To her, this is about more than the moment. It's about how safe she feels bringing things to you at all. It's about whether her emotional reality is treated like it matters — not just when she's calm and composed, but when she's hurt and frustrated and can't quite find the words. She wants to know: when I stop sounding pleasant, do you stop hearing me?

If you think she's "just being emotional," understand what you're actually saying. You're saying, "Your reaction makes me uncomfortable, so I'm going to reframe this conflict to make it about your instability instead of my behavior." You don't mean it that way — but that's how it lands. And it doesn't make her quieter. It makes her feel gaslit.

She starts wondering if you *ever* really listen. If your calm demeanor is actually disengagement. If you're using logic to avoid accountability. She might not be able to name that in the moment, but she feels it — and over time, that feeling calcifies into a belief: that she can't fight with you *and* feel seen at the same time.

That's where couples lose each other. Not in the argument itself, but in what the argument reveals. When she brings pain to the table, and your response is "That's not what happened," she's not going to double down. She's going to shut down. Or escalate. Or both.

You'll label it "drama." She'll label it "disconnection."

And around you go again.

Let's get something straight: *you're not more logical just because you're quieter.* You're not "better at conflict" just because you keep your voice down. Sometimes, your refusal to show emotion feels like stonewalling. And when you tell her she's "too emotional," what she hears is: *you're not allowed to be affected by things.*

You think you're de-escalating. She thinks you're disappearing.

So what does a good fight look like?

First, it starts with presence. Emotional presence. That means staying in the conversation even when it gets uncomfortable. Not pacing the room. Not staring at the ceiling. Not sighing every five seconds like she's interrupting your meditation retreat. Your nonverbal communication matters. If your posture is screaming, "I'm barely tolerating this," then it doesn't matter how carefully you phrase your sentences. She already feels shut out.

Second, stop managing the optics of the fight. You don't get points for staying calm if your calmness is just performative detachment. If she's crying and you're giving her the same tone you use with your phone company, you're not being mature — you're being emotionally evasive. You don't need to cry with her. You don't need to raise your voice. But you do need to *match the energy of sincerity.* That means eye contact. It means focus. It means responding to her emotions with emotional acknowledgment — not just statements of fact.

Let's say she says, "I feel like I do everything around here and you don't even notice." Your instinct might be to refute that. You'll want to say, "That's not true, I took the dog out and did the dishes and folded laundry on Sunday." But now you're defending a list. She's not mad about your performance record. She's mad about *feeling alone in the effort.*

A better response? "I didn't realize that's how it's been feeling for you. I know I've been caught up with work, and I want to understand what's been piling up on your side." That's not weakness. That's maturity. That's showing her you can hear her perspective *before* insisting on your own.

The other mistake men often make during fights is skipping the middle. You want to fix it fast. So once you feel like you've apologized — or explained your point — you're ready to move on. She's still talking. You're trying to close the tab.

This is where you need to slow down.

Fighting well doesn't mean resolving everything immediately. It means staying in the process long enough that both people feel heard. If she brings something up, don't treat it like a nuisance. Ask questions. Try to understand what's behind it. Was it just the thing that happened? Or was there a pattern that made it land harder?

You're not a bad husband because you messed up. But you do become harder to connect with when you act like every fight is a test she's failing — instead of a moment you're both responsible for managing better.

There's also this fun marital milestone: *the recycled argument.* You know the one. The fight that shows up wearing a new outfit but smells exactly like last year. It starts about weekend plans and ends with, "You never support me in front of your family." Or it begins with a harmless comment and turns into a referendum on how you always make her feel like the irrational one.

When this happens, don't say, "Why are we still talking about this?" Say, "This keeps coming up — I think we never really got to the root of it." That's how you change the story. Not by getting defensive, but by getting curious.

You don't need to agree with everything she says. But you do need to make space for it. Let her say the uncomfortable things. Don't cut her off. Don't correct her mid-sentence. Listen past the tone. Hear the fear. The fatigue. The need.

And when it's your turn, speak in full paragraphs — not sound bites. Don't use sarcasm. Don't toss in a joke to lighten the mood unless you're sure it will land. This isn't the time to be clever. It's the time to be *real.*

When you start treating fights not as interruptions to the relationship but as part of the relationship — when you stop rushing to fix and start learning how to *stay present in the mess* — everything gets better. She gets calmer. You feel less trapped. The arguments become less about who's right and more about what's true.

And yes, you'll still mess up. You'll still say the wrong thing, misread her tone, shut down too early, or think the issue is resolved when it isn't. But when she sees you trying to *fight better*, it gives her something to work with. Something to trust. Because now she's not the only one carrying the emotional labor of every hard conversation.

That shift is what she's really after. Not perfection. Participation. Not flawless communication, but *visible effort.*

She doesn't want you to agree with her all the time. She wants you to *respect the process* enough to take it seriously. And if you can do that — if you can learn to stay in the fight without weaponizing your calm or punishing her for feeling things deeply — she will start to believe that the relationship is a safe place to be honest.

That's what matters. Not who "wins." Not who has the cleanest logic. Not who stays composed the longest. But whether you're someone who listens, who adapts, and who stays close even when things are hard.

Because when she sees that, she'll stop dreading the next fight. She'll start believing in the one thing she's always wanted from you — not control, not compliance, but the knowledge that you can handle her *as she is,* even when the temperature rises.

And when that happens, she stops fighting to be heard. Because she finally knows you're actually there.

12: Mood Rings and Tripwires

(Why She Can Be Fine at Dinner and Crying in the Driveway — and What You're Missing)

It doesn't make sense to you. One minute she's laughing. The next she's distant. You had a nice dinner. She was making jokes. You thought everything was fine. Then something shifted. The air changed. Her voice got quieter. Her body language closed. You asked if something was wrong. She said no. But the way she looked at you said yes.

And now you're stuck — in the weird, echoey emotional cul-de-sac that every married man eventually learns to navigate: the sudden, unexpected shift in her mood that seems to come out of nowhere, with no instructions, no roadmap, and no obvious way back.

You didn't cause it — not directly. At least, you don't *think* you did. But now you're standing there, trying to figure out what just happened, while she's clearly having a moment and not saying much.

This, right here, is where a lot of men either check out or mess up. They get impatient. They ask once, then retreat when she doesn't answer. Or they jump to, "Well, if you're not going to tell me what's wrong, I can't help you," as if the problem is a customer service issue she's refusing to explain.

But what's happening isn't a mystery to her. It's just *layered.* What's happening is that she's processing something — something that may have started small but grew rapidly, usually fed by past experiences, unspoken fears, old disappointments, or a long list of things she's had to emotionally postpone until she had enough quiet to feel them all at once.

That quiet often shows up when you're present — when she's finally in a place where she feels emotionally safe enough to *not* smile through it. And instead of recognizing that as trust, you experience it as an emotional ambush.

Let's say you're on your way home from a gathering with friends. The night was light and easy. She made a few jokes. Laughed at someone's story. Gave you that look across the room that says, *I like being here with you.* On the drive back, you're feeling good — until she goes quiet. You ask what's wrong. She says, "Nothing."

But you can feel it — her silence is sharp around the edges. Something is definitely off.

What you don't realize is that something happened at that dinner party — a comment, a glance, maybe just a moment that stirred something in her. Something old. Maybe she felt invisible in a conversation. Maybe someone made a joke that hit a little too close to home. Maybe she saw something between another couple that triggered a sense of longing or comparison. She didn't say anything at the time — because she didn't want to "make a scene" or "overthink it."

But now you're alone. She has space. Her guard drops. And what you're seeing isn't her mood swinging like a pendulum — it's her actually *feeling* what she didn't have time or room to feel earlier.

This is hard for men to process. Because you tend to connect emotion with immediacy. If you're angry, it's probably about something that just happened. If you're sad, it's usually linked to a specific event. You don't keep emotional tabs open for hours or days, quietly waiting to download them when the Wi-Fi is better.

She does.

Her emotional world is layered and nonlinear. It's associative. A small thing now can open the door to a bigger thing from earlier. A passing moment can bring up something she hadn't thought about in weeks. That's not instability. That's emotional fluency.

You'll be tempted to say, "Just tell me what's wrong." Don't. At least, not like that. She may not *know* yet. Or she may know, but not have found a way to say it that won't sound "too big" or "too much." Or she may be testing — not in a manipulative way, but in a human way — whether you'll stay close when she's not easy.

And here's the hard part: a lot of men don't.

They check out. Get defensive. Go quiet. They feel like they're being emotionally baited into something they can't fix, so they back away. They make a joke. Or they grab their phone. Or they say, "Okay, just let me know when you want to talk," and disappear into another room.

That's not neutral. That's abandonment. Not in a dramatic, long-term way — but in the micro-moment where she needed closeness, and instead got distance.

So what should you do instead?

Stay. Even if she doesn't explain right away. Stay with her energy. Sit next to her. Ask softly, "Something's shifted — want to talk about it now, or later?" Make it clear you *noticed* the change, and you're not judging it. That alone can soften everything.

Don't demand clarity. Invite it. She may surprise you and open up quickly. Or she may need time. But what she's scanning for isn't a solution — it's whether you're safe to bring things to when she's still sorting them out.

Think about how you act when you're physically sick but not sure what's wrong. You want someone nearby. You don't want them poking you with questions or pushing you to perform wellness. You want quiet support. A hand. A presence. She wants the same when her emotional immune system is crashing. Not distance. Not pressure. Just steady proximity.

You may feel helpless in these moments. That's okay. It's not your job to fix her feelings. Your job is to make room for them.

And when she *does* begin to talk — really talk — your job is to *not interrupt.* Don't correct her timeline. Don't say, "That's not what happened." Don't remind her that she laughed at the time, or that someone else didn't mean anything by it. She knows all that. She doesn't need you to validate her logic. She needs you to trust her interpretation of her own emotional landscape.

This is where your listening muscles either grow — or collapse.

Because you'll want to jump in. You'll want to reassure. Defend. Fix. But what you really need to do is *hold space*. Nod. Ask for more if you don't understand something. Mirror back what you heard. And above all, don't rush her to a better mood just because her current one makes you uncomfortable.

She's not broken. She's feeling something.

Let her.

These "emotional whiplash" moments — where everything *seems* fine and then suddenly isn't — are usually not about manipulation or volatility. They're about emotional backlog. The stuff she couldn't process during the week, during the dinner, during the small talk. It comes out when she finally has bandwidth. And because she trusts *you*, it happens with you.

That's not a burden. That's access.

Now, let's talk about tripwires. These are the things you do — or don't do — that trigger her mood shift without you realizing it. You might say something that seems harmless, like "Relax," or "Why are you getting so worked up?" Or you might scroll your phone while she's talking, thinking you're still "listening." You might forget something she told you was important — not because you don't care, but because you didn't write it down or connect it to something that matters to you.

These tripwires aren't huge offenses. But they're pattern-confirmers. They quietly signal, *I'm not tracking with you emotionally.* And when they stack up, they make her mood feel less stable — not because she's erratic, but because you've given her less and less space to process openly.

Every woman has her own emotional tripwires. The one that says "Don't dismiss me." The one that says "Don't forget this again." The one that says "Don't make me feel invisible while I'm standing right here." You're not expected to know all of them up front. But you are expected to care enough to learn.

Ask her, when things are calm: "What's something I do that makes you feel like I'm not really there with you emotionally?" And then — this is key — don't defend yourself. Just listen. Take it in. You'll start to see that her mood shifts are not weather events. They're responses. Signals. Invitations, even.

When she's quiet, it's not always withdrawal. It's often testing. *Will you lean in, or will you retreat?*

When she's short with you, it's not always anger. It might be disappointment — that she had a moment to connect and you walked past it.

When she cries and says, "I don't know why I'm crying," she doesn't need you to figure it out. She needs you to stay nearby long enough that she doesn't have to explain it all alone.

That's what these moments are really about: *emotional proximity.* Are you close, not just physically, but energetically? Are you showing her, in tone and posture and choice, that she doesn't have to earn your attention with perfect timing or perfect composure?

If the answer is yes — if you can be that kind of steady, available presence — she won't stop feeling things. But she'll stop feeling like she has to hide them. And when that happens, when she finally relaxes into knowing she doesn't have to manage your comfort every time her emotions shift, your connection deepens in ways you won't see coming. Because that trust — the kind that says *he'll still be here when I get quiet, when I get overwhelmed, when I'm not easy* — is what transforms emotional volatility into emotional safety. Not through perfectly managed conversations or a flawless sense of timing, but through quiet consistency. Through your ability to stay close without needing to solve everything. To witness what she feels without making it about you. That's the kind of presence that builds intimacy beneath the surface — not just when things are light, but when they're complicated. And it's in those quiet, confusing, emotionally layered moments — the ones that used to make you withdraw — that she'll finally believe you know how to stay.

13: The Memory Vault

(Why She Remembers Every Fight, Word, and Look — and What It's Really About)

There will come a moment in your marriage — possibly in the middle of a disagreement that started over nothing — when she says something like, "This is just like what happened at your sister's house last year."

You'll pause. Blink. Try to remember what happened at your sister's house last year.

You'll come up with nothing.

And that's when you'll realize: *you're in a fight about a fight you don't remember.*

She remembers it, though. In detail. She remembers what you were wearing, what you said, how you said it, who else was there, and exactly how it made her feel. She's not making it up. She's not holding a grudge for fun. She just has a memory like a digital voice recorder attached to her emotional experiences — and yes, it's still recording.

You, meanwhile, move through the world with a kind of practical amnesia. You remember categories — that you had an argument, or that something was "tense for a while" — but not the play-by-play. Not the tone. Not the expression on her face when she said, "I'm done trying to explain this to you." Not the way she went quiet in the car, or how she turned away that night when you reached for her.

She cataloged it. You barely filed it.

This discrepancy doesn't mean she's obsessive. It doesn't mean you're careless. But it *does* mean your brains — and your priorities — work differently. And if you don't recognize that difference, you're going to spend a lot of time thinking she's "bringing up old stuff" just to win arguments. She's not. She's bringing up emotional data you discarded, and that's not petty. That's what her brain was trained to do.

See, women are often raised to track emotion. They're taught to notice shifts in mood, tone, posture, context. They're socialized to monitor not just what's happening but how it's *landing.* And when something lands badly — when a moment hurts, confuses, or isolates them — it sticks.

You, on the other hand, were raised to move on. To resolve. To minimize. To bounce back. Maybe you said something awful during a fight, but you apologized, made up, and assumed it was behind you. That's what men are taught. Compartmentalize. Put it in the past. Done.

Except she's not done. She forgave, maybe. But she didn't forget. Not because she's looking to reopen the wound — but because *you never actually cleaned it out.*

You said you were sorry. But did you understand why it hurt? Did you ask what made it linger? Did you acknowledge the emotional impact, or did you just go through the motions, hoping she'd stop being upset?

Here's the hard truth: *every time you downplay something she's still holding onto, you teach her that her memory is a liability.* That being honest about how something felt makes her "too sensitive" or "unable to let things go." And the moment she starts believing that, she stops trusting that you care about her full experience — not just the version you're comfortable with.

Let's talk about how this shows up in real life.

Maybe she brings up the way you joked about her in front of your friends last Christmas. You barely remember it. To you, it was just a quick laugh, nothing personal. But to her, it was loaded. It made her feel exposed. Mocked. You were playing to your audience, and she felt like collateral.

Or maybe she still feels off about the way you snapped at her before a family dinner six months ago. You were stressed, sure, but she was looking forward to that night. She had made an effort, picked the place, gotten dressed up. And your mood slammed the brakes on the evening before it even started. You think, *We got through it.* She thinks, *You still don't know how much that stung.*

Or maybe it's the one argument you thought was "just a rough patch," but she remembers it as the night she stopped feeling safe bringing up hard things. You didn't yell. You just shut down. You made her feel like her pain was a problem to solve or silence — not something you could sit with. She remembers that because it changed how she saw you. How she saw *talking* to you.

This is the memory vault. It's not a weapon. It's not a trap. It's not a threat. It's the archive of how she experiences you — how you show up, how you disappear, how you recover, and how you remember (or don't).

The biggest mistake men make is treating that vault like a storage unit she's supposed to empty every few months. But memory isn't clutter to her. It's context.

She keeps it because it helps her track whether she's being heard, loved, prioritized — or just tolerated.

And no, she doesn't expect you to remember every detail. She knows your brain doesn't work like that. But she *does* expect you to care that hers does.

That means when she brings something up, even if it feels ancient, you don't say, "You're still mad about that?" You say, "I honestly didn't realize that stuck with you — can you tell me what part of it still feels raw?"

And then — listen. Not to win. Not to move on. But to understand. You don't need to agree with her version of events. But you do need to understand *her version of experience.*

You also need to stop treating memory like an accusation. When she says, "This reminds me of when you blew off our anniversary two years ago," she's not saying, "You're a terrible person." She's saying, "I've been here before — and I'm afraid you didn't learn from it."

Women use memory the way you use logic. To track patterns. To stay safe. To decide what kind of emotional risk is acceptable. If she starts pulling up past events, that's not spite. That's self-protection.

Here's where things get trickier: sometimes *you* remember things, but you remember them differently. You remember the tone being fine. You remember her saying it was okay. You remember the fight ending with a hug and a joke.

And now she's saying she never felt heard.

Your instinct will be to argue. To correct the record. To prove that she's remembering it "wrong."

Don't.

Memory is not a courtroom transcript. It's not a replay. It's a *felt* thing. Her memory isn't just about what happened. It's about what she experienced. And if you try to debate her feelings like a technicality, you will lose — not just the argument, but something deeper: her willingness to keep telling you how things land with her at all.

When she tells you what she remembers, that's vulnerability. She's pulling something out of the vault and letting you examine it. You don't have to agree with the entire account. But you do have to treat it with care.

This doesn't mean you have to live under constant threat of "emotional recall." She's not going to throw every mistake back in your face during every disagreement — unless she feels like you never actually learned anything. If the same wounds keep reappearing, ask yourself why.

Are you repeating patterns without noticing? Are you offering shallow apologies to get through the moment?

Are you refusing to connect the dots between how you act and how she responds?

Memory isn't the problem. The pattern is.

But here's the good news: memory can also work in your favor.

She remembers when you showed up. When you fixed something without being asked. When you defended her in a room where she felt alone. When you made her laugh after a hard week. When you asked how her meeting went — not because she reminded you, but because you *listened* the first time.

She holds on to that stuff. She just doesn't always *lead* with it — because her nervous system is tracking safety, and her memory prioritizes threat. That's biology. That's wiring. It doesn't mean she doesn't see your goodness. It just means she's more likely to bring up the time you disappeared emotionally than the time you remembered to grab her favorite wine. Both mattered. But one still feels unfinished.

If you want her to let go of the past, don't tell her to forget it. Show her something new. Offer a different pattern. A different response. Show her that you don't just want to "move on" — you want to *move forward*, with awareness.

When she brings something out of the vault, handle it like a fragile object. Not because she's fragile — but because what she's showing you is something she's held onto, alone, for longer than she should've had to. She didn't bring it up to rehash. She brought it up hoping you'd say, "I see now why that mattered. I didn't see it then, but I'm here now."

That sentence, delivered sincerely, does more than any defensive rebuttal or tidy apology ever could. Because it doesn't erase her memory. It *redeems* it. And once her memory stops being a storage unit for unresolved tension, it becomes a library of trust — a record of all the times you've shown her you're still learning, still listening, still here.

And when she sees you treat her memory not as a weapon, but as a guide, she'll stop bracing for the moment you tell her she's "bringing up old stuff again." She'll start believing you finally understand why she remembers it — and what it means to her that you didn't forget.

14: Security Clearance
(Why She's Not Needy — She Just Needs to Know You're Safe)

If you haven't figured it out yet, your wife is not asking you for constant reassurance because she's insecure. She's asking because she's watching. Not your words — your consistency. Your follow-through. Your emotional posture. Your choices when you think she's not looking. She's not looking for perfection. She's looking for safety.

You might think, *I've never given her a reason not to trust me.* But from her perspective, the absence of cheating or lying isn't the same thing as emotional safety. That's just *not screwing up.* Safety is something else entirely. It's about knowing that she doesn't have to brace herself — not just for betrayal, but for dismissal, distance, deflection, or neglect.

It's knowing you won't shut down in a hard conversation. That you won't retreat into silence every time she's upset. That when she says, "I need you to hear this," you don't get defensive or go cold. That when she shares something vulnerable — something raw — you don't make a joke, change the subject, or disappear behind a glazed-over stare.

It's not that she's asking you to fix her life. She's asking you to not add more uncertainty to it. To not become one more thing she has to interpret, manage, tiptoe around, or carry.

You may hear her use words like "safe" or "secure" and think, *What does that even mean?* You haven't cheated. You haven't lied. You don't scream or throw things. Isn't that safe enough?

No.

That's a low bar. That's like saying a house is "safe" because it hasn't burned down yet. She's looking for a home, not just a structure that hasn't collapsed. She wants to know that what you build together can weather stress. That it has insulation. That it won't leak the first time there's emotional pressure.

Women are biologically and socially wired to assess safety constantly — especially with the people closest to them. That's not paranoia. That's pattern recognition.

She's scanning for small cues. Micro-signals. Is he present? Is he here with me in this moment, or is he three feet away but emotionally off the grid? Is he listening, or is he nodding while waiting to exit the conversation? Does he hear me the first time, or do I have to escalate before he tunes in?

She's not doing this to trap you. She's doing this because she's learned that when a man starts to withdraw — even subtly — it's often a sign of something bigger. Not cheating. Not betrayal. Just emotional evacuation. That slow slide into surface-level conversations and logistical texts and "we're fine" status reports while the real closeness slowly erodes.

And yes, she might bring it up. She might say, "You've felt far away lately." And if you say, "I've just been tired," she'll nod — but what she's thinking is, *I've been tired too, and I'm still here. Still showing up.*

She's not measuring your exhaustion. She's measuring your availability. Are you reachable when it matters? Do you notice when she's quiet? Do you follow up when she says she's overwhelmed — or do you assume she'll bounce back because she always does?

Safety isn't grand gestures. It's subtle proof. Small consistencies. It's texting when you're running late without being reminded. It's checking in on her big day without waiting for her to prompt you. It's not asking for credit every time you do what's expected.

When she feels unsafe — not in a physical sense, but in the sense that she can't fully relax around you — it doesn't always show up as fear. Sometimes it looks like irritation. Like distance. Like she's over-managing everything and won't let you in. You think she's being controlling. She thinks she's holding the relationship together while you zone out.

Here's where men often miss the mark: they think safety means not doing bad things. But for her, it means doing *reliable* things. Predictably. Without drama. Without needing to be chased for answers or reminded twice. You say you'll take care of it, and she knows that means it will actually get done. You say you'll be somewhere at six, and she doesn't have to build a contingency plan just in case.

You might think she's overreacting when she brings up that time you dropped the ball on something minor — forgot to pay a bill, spaced on a plan, missed a date night reservation. But it's not about the task. It's about the ripple effect. She's been trained to see those small gaps as a warning: if she doesn't track it, it might fall apart. If she doesn't remind you, she might get burned. And once that mindset settles in, it's hard to shake.

Want to build her trust faster than flowers or apologies ever could? Start noticing. Anticipate. Be early. Be consistent. Don't let things slide and then act surprised that she's upset. Let her see that your word has weight. That she doesn't have to double-check your intentions, your attention, or your basic responsibilities.

And when she brings up a time she *didn't* feel safe, don't make her regret it. Don't get defensive. Don't make it about your feelings. You're allowed to have your own reaction — but not at the cost of hers. If she says, "That moment really hurt," and your instinct is to say, "That's not what I meant," you've missed the whole point. She's not asking you to correct her. She's asking you to care.

She knows you're human. She knows you're not going to get it right all the time. But she's watching how you respond to the moments when she says, "This landed wrong," or "That scared me," or "I felt really alone."

Do you lean in? Or do you push back?

The moment you start making her emotions about your inconvenience, she stops showing them to you. And from that point forward, every fight gets harder. Because now she's not just arguing about what happened — she's arguing against the belief that you won't hear her even if she explains it perfectly.

It's exhausting for her to have to ask for what she thought would be obvious: *Be dependable. Be present. Be easy to reach — not just by phone, but emotionally. Show up without needing to be dragged.*

You don't have to be a therapist. You don't have to be a soft-spoken monk. You just have to stop acting like her needs are some unsolvable mystery.

Most of the time, what she needs is this: to know that if something goes wrong — with the house, the bills, the kids, her job, her body, her heart — you won't vanish. You won't make it worse. You won't mock or minimize or act like she's being dramatic. You'll stay close. Listen. Respond. Adapt. Not just once, but consistently. And you'll do it not because she's fragile — but because she's valuable.

This is what makes a man feel *safe* to a woman. Not the size of his bank account. Not his job title. Not even his ability to "fix" things. It's his presence. His emotional steadiness. His ability to take things seriously without making them heavy. His ability to witness her in her realness — frustration, vulnerability, contradiction — and not flinch.

If she's asking for more communication, it's because she doesn't want to guess what mood you're in. If she wants you to check in during the day, it's because she wants to feel remembered, not micromanaged. If she's upset you didn't follow through, it's not because she wanted to nag — it's because now *she* has to deal with the consequences of something you said you'd handle.

That's not neediness. That's lived experience.

And here's the secret you don't hear enough: when she *does* feel safe with you — when she doesn't have to manage your moods or double-check your intentions — everything else softens. Her tone. Her patience. Her affection. Her defenses. When she believes, deep in her bones, that she's not alone in holding the weight of this shared life, she doesn't feel the need to raise her voice just to be heard.

She relaxes. And when she relaxes, she lets you in more. She trusts you with the parts of herself she's had to protect in other relationships — or even in this one, before you figured this stuff out.

That trust isn't built in grand romantic gestures. It's built in how you handle Wednesday night when she's overwhelmed, and whether you notice without being told. It's built in whether you remember what she said three days ago, and follow up — not for points, but because you *give a damn.*

And if you're thinking, *This all sounds like a lot*, that's fair. It *is* a lot — not because women are too demanding, but because most men have never been taught how to carry this kind of weight. You were taught to show up, provide, protect — but not how to *stay* emotionally close when someone else is falling apart.

She's not asking for magic. She's asking for maturity. For shared emotional responsibility. For a relationship where she can finally let down her guard because she trusts that when things get hard, you'll be standing right next to her — not somewhere else waiting for her to "get over it."

That kind of emotional security is rare. But once she knows she has it, she won't just love you more. She'll start showing you parts of herself you didn't even know she was holding back. Not because she was testing you — but because she needed to be sure you wouldn't drop her once she let go.

15: Still Her Boyfriend

(Why "Husband" Isn't the Final Promotion — and What She Still Needs From You)

You did it. You won her over. She said yes. You got the ring, the ceremony, the photos, the license. And now you're married — officially, legally, permanently hers. You exhaled. You relaxed. You settled into the role.

And that, right there, is where the problem starts.

Because for a lot of men, "husband" feels like a promotion. A conclusion. A job title you now hold for life. You put in the work, made the grand gesture, committed to the relationship, and now the partnership is established. You've graduated.

But for her, "husband" isn't the destination. It's just the beginning.

See, in your mind, the courtship phase is over. You don't need to charm her anymore. You don't need to plan dates, write notes, leave little surprises, or flirt in text messages. You're married now. You made it.

To her, that logic feels like emotional bait and switch. Because she didn't fall in love with a husband. She fell in love with a *boyfriend* — someone who pursued her. Who noticed things. Who asked questions and didn't act like he already had her all figured out. Who flirted in the kitchen, reached for her hand in public, sent ridiculous GIFs and asked what she wanted for dinner without sounding bored.

She misses him.

You may not have noticed it happening — the shift from boyfriend to administrator. From eager to efficient. From "What do you feel like doing tonight?" to "We need to talk about the lawn guy." You're not being cold. You're just in logistics mode. You're solving. Managing. Checking boxes. But somewhere in that transition, she stopped feeling *seen.*

And when a woman stops feeling seen, she doesn't complain about the flowers you don't buy. She doesn't say, "I wish you'd look at me like you did when we were dating." Instead, she gets quiet. She retreats into roles — partner, roommate, co-parent, scheduler, budget manager. She keeps the machine running. But emotionally? She starts to go dark.

You won't even notice at first. She still kisses you goodnight. Still helps clean up the kitchen. Still reminds you about your mom's birthday. But she's not sharing herself the same way. Not reaching for you as often. Not lighting up when you walk in the room. Not texting during the day just to say something dumb and sweet.

And you'll assume it's just life. That this is what marriage *is* after a while — functional, adult, low-flame but steady. You'll shrug off the shift like it's just a symptom of work, routine, or tiredness. You won't realize that she's pulling back because she no longer feels like the woman you *want.* She feels like the woman you *have.*

That distinction matters more than you think.

Women don't just want love. They want to feel *chosen* — not once, but over and over. They want to know that if you met them again today, you'd still pursue them. Still flirt. Still work to win them. Still show curiosity, effort, intentionality — all the things you did when nothing was guaranteed.

You may think, *She knows I love her. She knows I'm not going anywhere.* And that's probably true. But what you're describing is stability — not intimacy. And intimacy fades when it's not actively tended.

Here's where the myth of "low-maintenance" becomes a trap. You may have told yourself that she's chill. That she doesn't need grand gestures. That she's not one of those women who needs attention all the time. That she's cool with takeout and sweats and forgetting the anniversary dinner because she "gets it."

What you missed is that the reason she's low-maintenance is because she *stopped expecting more.*

Not because she doesn't want more. But because you trained her not to.

And the longer you go without showing her that you still see her as someone to pursue, the more she adapts. Not in a dramatic, "I'm leaving you" way. But in small, steady withdrawals. She gives less of herself emotionally. She shares fewer thoughts that don't serve a purpose. She stops looking at you in that way she used to — not because she doesn't love you, but because it feels like a waste of emotional energy to aim it where it's no longer reflected.

That's what emotional withdrawal looks like. Not loud. Not explosive. Just... *less.*

Less flirtation. Less touch. Less play. Less eye contact. Less reaching across the room because it's been weeks since you reached first.

And if you try to address it later — when she's already half-gone emotionally — you'll be stunned at how much she's held in. She'll say things like, "I feel like we're just roommates," or "I don't think you even *see* me anymore." And you'll think, *Where did this come from?* But it didn't come out of nowhere. It came out of every moment where you acted like keeping her meant you didn't need to *keep choosing* her.

So what does it look like to be her boyfriend *after* you become her husband?

It doesn't mean buying jewelry or booking surprise trips. Those things are fine. But they're not the point. The point is effort. The point is making her feel like she's not just *in* your life, but *at the center* of it.

It means texting her during the day — not to ask what time dinner is, but just to say you were thinking about her. It means reaching for her when you walk by, even if the kids are around. It means complimenting her in real-time, not waiting for an occasion. It means asking how she's feeling, and actually sitting still long enough to hear the answer. It means making plans — actual plans, not vague "we should do something soon" talk — and following through.

It also means studying her again. Not assuming you know everything about her because you've shared a bathroom for six years. Ask new questions. Find out what's changed. What's she curious about lately? What does she wish she had more time for? What's making her feel powerful — or powerless — in this season?

Dating your wife isn't a corny rom-com punchline. It's emotional maintenance. It's a relational discipline. And the couples who do it — who prioritize each other not just in name, but in *action* — are the ones who don't wake up one day feeling like they're strangers who happen to share a mortgage.

Because here's the truth: someone will notice her if you stop. Someone will flirt. Someone will ask questions. Someone will remind her that she's magnetic. And if she no longer feels that from you — if she starts feeling more alive in the presence of other people than in yours — it won't always lead to cheating. But it will lead to distance. Loneliness. And eventually, resignation.

It's not jealousy that keeps a marriage connected. It's *engagement.* And engagement comes from intentional effort — not because you're afraid of losing her, but because you *want* her to know she still lights you up.

And before you panic — no, this doesn't mean daily poetry readings and foot rubs and color-coded date night calendars. It just means that you show her, regularly and deliberately, that she still holds your gaze. That she's not just your partner in logistics, but the woman who still turns your head and pulls you closer for no reason at all.

You were good at this once. You didn't get married without being good at it. The problem isn't that you can't be romantic or expressive. The problem is that you filed that version of yourself under "Dating Behavior" and assumed you didn't need it anymore once the ring was on.

But she didn't fall in love with your title. She fell in love with your *attention.*

And if you're still that man — or willing to become him again — you'll be amazed at what opens back up between you. Not just sex (though yes, that too), but *availability.* Warmth. Playfulness. She'll show you more of herself — not because you demanded it, but because she *feels* it's safe again to be that open, that silly, that soft.

It's not about proving something. It's about remembering how to see her. The way you did in the beginning. Not because she's new, but because she's *still* worth that gaze.

And when she sees that look again — that spark of recognition, of desire, of delight — something shifts. She relaxes. She softens. She comes closer. Not because she has to. But because she feels, for the first time in a long time, like your girlfriend again. Like the woman who made your stomach flip just by walking into the room. Like the woman you couldn't stop texting. Like the one who still wants you, but needs to know you still want her too — not out of habit, but out of *choice.* The kind you keep making every single day.

About the Author

Faye Clifton believes that relationships are messy, hilarious, and occasionally held together with equal parts love, compromise, and duct tape. Raised in a household where good manners mattered and emotional intelligence was an unspoken requirement, she learned early that living with someone — really *living* with them — takes more than shared chores and mutual attraction. It takes perspective. Humor. Patience. And sometimes the ability to walk away from an argument long enough to come back with snacks.

She's the author of *Sparkling Clean: The Ultimate Guide to Mastering Dishwashing* and *DIY to "I Do": The Bride's Sanity-Saving Wedding Planner*, two favorite reads among first-time brides, bridesmaids, shower guests, and anyone who finds beauty in the absurdity of adult life.

Faye writes books for women — but every once in a while, she turns the table and writes something *for* men. This book is her way of offering a little honest guidance, a little encouragement, and a loving nudge in the right direction.

She lives somewhere quiet, keeps her dish towels folded in thirds, and is happily married to someone who still makes her laugh on purpose.

Made in the USA
Middletown, DE
27 May 2025